Tertullian

To His Wife

Tertullian

To His Wife

Tertullian
To His Wife

Published by
Lighthouse Christian Publishing
SAN 257-4330
5531 Dufferin Drive
Savage, Minnesota, 55378
United States of America

www.lighthousechristianpublishing.com

Tertullian

To His Wife.

Book I.

Chapter I.—Design of the Treatise. Disavowal of Personal Motives in Writing It.

I have thought it meet, my best beloved fellow-servant in the Lord, even from this early period, to provide for the course which you must pursue after my departure from the world, if I shall be called before you; (and) to entrust to your honor the observance of the provision. For in things worldly we are active enough, and we wish the good of each of us to be consulted. If we draw up wills for *such* matters, why ought we not much more to take forethought for our posterity in things divine and heavenly, and in a sense to bequeath a legacy to be received before the inheritance be divided, — (the legacy, I mean, of) admonition and demonstration touching those (bequests) which are allotted out of (our) immortal goods, and from the heritage of the heavens? Only, that you may be able to receive in its entirety this feoffment in trust of my admonition, may God grant; to whom be honor, glory, renown, dignity, and power, now and to the ages of the ages!

The precept, therefore, which I give you is, that, with all the constancy you may, you do, after our departure, renounce nuptials; not that you will on that score confer any benefit on me, except in that you will profit yourself. But to Christians, after their departure from the world, no restoration of marriage is promised in the day of the resurrection, translated as they will be into the condition and sanctity of angels. Therefore, no solicitude arising from carnal jealousy will, in the day of the resurrection, even in the case of her whom they chose to represent as having been married to seven brothers successively, wound any one of her so many husbands; nor is any (husband) awaiting her to put her to confusion. The question raised by the Sadducees has yielded to the Lord's sentence. Think not that it is for the sake of preserving to the end for myself the entire devotion of your flesh, that I, suspicious of the pain of (anticipated) slight, am even at this early period instilling into you the counsel of (perpetual) widowhood. There will at that day be no resumption of voluptuous disgrace between us. No such frivolities, no such impurities, does God promise to His (servants). But whether to you, or to any other woman whatever who pertains to God, the advice which we are giving shall be profitable, we take leave to treat of at large.

Chapter II. —Marriage Lawful, But Not Polygamy.

We do not indeed forbid the union of man and woman, blest by God as the seminary of the human race, and devised for the replenishment of the earth and the furnishing of the world, and therefore permitted, yet singly. For Adam was the one husband of Eve, and Eve his one wife, one woman, one rib. We grant, that among our ancestors, and the patriarchs themselves, it was lawful not only to marry, but even to multiply wives. There were concubines, too, (in those days.)

But although the Church did come in figuratively in the synagogue, yet (to interpret simply) it was necessary to institute (certain things) which should afterward deserve to be either lopped off or modified. For the Law was (in due time) to supervene. (Nor was that enough:) for it was meet that causes for making up the deficiencies of the Law should have forerun (Him who was to supply those deficiencies). And so to the Law presently had to succeed the Word of God introducing the spiritual circumcision. Therefore, by means of the wide license of those days, materials for subsequent emendations were furnished beforehand, of which materials the Lord by His Gospel, and then the apostle in the last days of the (Jewish) age, either cut off the redundancies or regulated the disorders.

Chapter III. —Marriage Good: Celibacy Preferable.

But let it not be thought that my reason for premising thus much concerning the liberty granted to the old, and the restraint imposed on the later time, is that I may lay a foundation for teaching that Christ's advent was intended to dissolve wedlock, (and) to abolish marriage talons; as if from this period onward I were prescribing an end to marrying. Let them see to that, who, among the rest of their perversities, teach the disjoining of the "one flesh in twain;" denying Him who, after borrowing the female from the male, recombined between themselves, in the matrimonial computation, the two bodies taken out of the consort ship of the self-same material substance. In short, there is no place at all where we read that nuptials are prohibited; of course on the ground that they are "a good thing." What, however, is *better* than this "good," we learn from the apostle, who *permits* marrying indeed, but *prefers* abstinence; the former on account of the insidiousnesses of temptations, the latter on account of the straits of the times. Now, by looking into the reason thus given for each proposition, it is easily discerned that the ground on which the power of marrying is conceded is *necessity*; but whatever *necessity* grants, she by her very nature depreciates. In fact, in that it is written, "To marry is better than to burn," what, pray, is the nature of this "good" which is (only) commended by comparison with "evil," so that the reason why "marrying" is *more* good is (merely) that "burning" is *less*? Nay, but how far better is it neither to marry nor to burn? Why, even in persecutions it is *better* to take advantage of the permission granted, and "flee from town to town," than, when apprehended and racked, to deny (the faith). And therefore more blessed are they who have strength to depart (this life) in blessed confession of their testimony. I may say, what is *permitted* is not *good*. For how stands the case? I must of necessity die (if I be apprehended and confess my faith.) If I think (that fate) deplorable, (then flight) is good; but if I have a fear of the thing which is permitted, (the permitted thing) has some suspicion attaching to the cause of its permission. But that which is "better" no one (ever) "permitted," as being undoubted, and manifest by its own inherent purity. There are some things which are not to be *desired* merely because they are not *forbidden*, albeit they are in a certain sense *forbidden* when other things are preferred to them; for the preference given to the higher things is a dissuasion from the lowest. A thing is not "good" merely because it is not "evil," nor is it "evil" merely because it is not "harmful." Further: that which is fully "good" excels on this ground, that it is not only not harmful, but profitable into the bargain. For you are bound to prefer what is profitable to what is (merely) not harmful. For the *first* place is what every struggle aims at; the *second* has consolation attaching to it, but not victory. But if we listen to the apostle, forgetting what is behind, let us both strain after what is before, and be followers after the better rewards. Thus, albeit he does not "cast a snare upon us," he points out what tends to utility when he says, "The unmarried woman thinks on the things of the Lord, that both in body and spirit she may be holy; but the married is solicitous how to please her husband."

But he nowhere permits marriage in such a way as not rather to wish us to do our utmost in imitation of his own example. Happy the man who shall prove like Paul!

Chapter IV. —Of the Infirmity of the Flesh, and Similar Pleas.

But we read "that the flesh is weak;" and hence we soothe ourselves in some cases. Yet we read, too, that "the spirit is strong;" for each clause occurs in one and the same sentence. Flesh is an earthly, spirit a heavenly, material. Why, then, do we, too prone to self-excuse, put forward (in our defense) the weak part of us, but not look at the strong? Why should not the earthly yield to the heavenly? If the spirit is stronger than the flesh, because it is withal of nobler origin, it is our own fault if we follow the weaker. Now there are two phases of human weakness which make marriages necessary to such as are disjoined from matrimony. The first and most powerful is that which arises from *fleshly* concupiscence; the second, from *worldly* concupiscence. But by us, who are servants of God, who renounce both voluptuousness and ambition, each is to be repudiated. Fleshly concupiscence claims the functions of adult age, craves after beauty's harvest, rejoices in its own shame, pleads the necessity of a husband to the female sex, as a source of authority and of comfort, or to render it safe from evil rumors. To meet these its counsels, do you apply the examples of sisters of ours whose names are with the Lord, —who, when their husbands have preceded them (to glory), give to no opportunity of beauty or of age the precedence over holiness. They prefer to be wedded to God. To God their beauty, to God their youth (is dedicated). With Him they live; with Him they converse; Him they "handle" by day\ and by night; *to* the Lord they assign their prayers as dowries; *from* Him, as oft as they desire it, they receive His approbation as dotal gifts. Thus they have laid hold for themselves of an eternal gift of the Lord; and while on earth, by abstaining from marriage, are already counted as belonging to the angelic family. Training yourself to an emulation of (their) constancy by the examples of such women, you will by spiritual affection bury that fleshly concupiscence, in abolishing the temporal and fleeting desires of beauty and youth by the compensating gain of immortal blessings.

On the other hand, this *worldly* concupiscence (to which I referred) has, as its causes, glory, cupidity, ambition, want of sufficiency; through which causes it trumps up the "necessity" for marrying, —promising itself, forsooth, heavenly things in return—to lord it, (namely,) in another's family; to roost on another's wealth; to extort splendor from another's store to lavish expenditure which you do not feel! Far be all this from believers, who have no care about maintenance, unless it be that we distrust the promises of God, and (His) care and providence, who clothes with such grace the lilies of the field; who, without any labor on their part, feeds the fowls of the heaven; who prohibits care to be taken about to-morrow's food and clothing, promising that He knows what is needful for each of His servants—not indeed ponderous necklaces, not burdensome garments, not Gallic mules nor German bearers, which all add luster to the glory of nuptials; but "sufficiency," which is suitable to moderation and modesty. Presume, I pray you, that you have need of nothing if you "attend upon the Lord;" nay, that you have all things, if you have the Lord, whose are all things. Think often on things heavenly, and you will despise things earthly. To widowhood signed and sealed before the Lord naught is necessary but perseverance.

Chapter V.—Of the Love of Offspring as a Plea for Marriage.

Further reasons for marriage which men allege for themselves arise from anxiety for posterity, and the bitter, bitter pleasure of children. To *us* this is idle. For why should we be eager to bear children, whom, when we have them, we desire to send before us (to glory) (in respect, I mean, of the distresses that are now imminent); desirous as we are ourselves, too, to be taken out of this most wicked world, and received into the Lord's presence, which was the desire even of an apostle? To the servant of God, forsooth, offspring is necessary! For of our own salvation we are secure enough, so that we have leisure for children! Burdens must be sought by us for ourselves which are avoided even by the majority of the Gentiles, who are compelled by laws, who are decimated by abortions; burdens which, finally, are to *us* most of all unsuitable, as being perilous to faith! For why did the Lord foretell a "woe to them that are with child, and them that give suck," except because He testifies that in that day of disencumbrance the encumbrances of children will be an inconvenience? It is to marriage, of course, that those encumbrances appertain; but that ("woe") will not pertain to widows. (*They*) at the first trump of the angel will spring forth disencumbered—will freely bear to the end whatsoever pressure and persecution, with no burdensome fruit of marriage heaving in the womb, none in the bosom.

Therefore, whether it be for the sake of the flesh, or of the world, or of posterity, that marriage is undertaken, nothing of all these "necessities" affects the servants of God, so as to prevent my deeming it enough to have once for all yielded to some one of them, and by one marriage appeased all concupiscence of this kind. Let us marry daily, and in the midst of our marrying let us be overtaken, like Sodom and Gomorrah, by that day of fear! For *there* it was not only, of course, that they were dealing in marriage and merchandise; but when He says, "They were marrying and buying," He sets a brand upon the very leading vices of the flesh and of the world, which call men off the most from divine disciplines—the one through the pleasure of rioting, the other though the greed of acquiring. And yet that "blindness" *then* was felt long before "the ends of the world." What, then, will the case be if God *now* keep us from the vices which *of old* were detestable before Him? "The time," says (the apostle), "is compressed. It remaineth that they who have wives act as if they had them not."

Chapter VI. —Examples of Heathens Urged as Commendatory of Widowhood and Celibacy.

But if they who *have* (wives) are (thus) bound to consign to oblivion what they have, how much more are they who have *not*, prohibited from seeking a second time what they no longer have; so that she whose husband has departed from the world should thenceforward impose rest on her sex by abstinence from marriage—abstinence which numbers of Gentile women devote to the memory of beloved husbands! When anything seems difficult, let us survey others who cope with still greater difficulties. How many are there who from the moment of their baptism set the seal (of virginity) upon their flesh? How many, again, who by equal mutual consent cancel the debt of matrimony—voluntary eunuchs for the sake of their desire after the celestial kingdom! But if, while the marriage-tie is still intact, abstinence is endured, how much more when it has been undone! For I believe it to be harder for what is intact to be quite forsaken, than for what has been lost not to be yearned after. A hard and arduous thing enough, surely, is the continence for God's sake of a holy woman after her husband's decease, when Gentiles, in honor of their own Satan, endure sacerdotal offices which involve both virginity and widowhood! At Rome, for instance, they who have to do with the type of that "inextinguishable fire," keeping watch over the omens of their own (future) penalty, in company with the (old) dragon himself, are appointed on the ground of *virginity*. To the Achæan Juno, at the town Ægium, a *virgin* is allotted; and the (priestesses) who rave at Delphi know not marriage. Moreover, we know that *widows* minister to the African Ceres; enticed away, indeed, from matrimony by a most stem oblivion: for not only do they withdraw from their still living husbands, but they even introduce other wives to them in their own room—the husbands, of course, smiling on it—all contact (with males), even as far as the kiss of their sons, being forbidden them; and yet, with enduring practice, they persevere in such a discipline of widowhood, which excludes the solace even of holy affection. These precepts have the devil given to his servants, and he is heard! He challenges, forsooth, God's servants, by the continence of his own, as if on equal terms! Continent are even the priests of hell! For he has found a way to ruin men even in good pursuits; and with him it makes no difference to slay some by voluptuousness, some by continence.

Chapter VII. —The Death of a Husband is God's Call to the Widow to Continence. Further Evidences from Scripture and from Heathenism.

To us continence has been pointed out by the Lord of salvation as an instrument for attaining eternity, and as a testimony of (our) faith; as a commendation of this flesh of ours, which is to be sustained for the "garment of immortality," which is one day to supervene; for enduring, in fine, the will of God. Besides, reflect, I advise you, that there is no one who is taken out of the world but by the will of God, if, (as is the case,) not even a leaf falls from off a tree without it. The same who brings us into the world must of necessity take us out of it too. Therefore, when, through the will of God, the husband is deceased, the marriage likewise, by the will of God, deceases. Why should *you* restore what God has put an end to? Why do you, by repeating the servitude of matrimony, spurn the liberty which is offered you? "You have been bound to a wife," says the apostle; "seek not loosing. You have been loosed from a wife; seek not binding." For even if you do not "*sin*" in remarrying, still he says "pressure of the flesh ensues." Wherefore, so far as we can, let us love the opportunity of continence; as soon as it offers itself, let us resolve to accept it, that what we have not had strength (to follow) in matrimony

we may follow in widowhood. The occasion must be embraced which puts an end to that which *necessity* commanded.
How detrimental to faith, how obstructive to holiness, second marriages are, the discipline of the Church and the prescription of the apostle declare, when he suffers not men twice married to preside (over a Church), when he would not grant a widow admittance into the order unless she had been "the wife of one man;" for it behooves God's altar to be set forth pure. That whole halo which encircles the Church is represented (as consisting) of holiness. Priesthood is (a function) of widowhood and of celibacies among the nations. Of course (this is) in conformity with the devil's principle of rivalry. For the king of heathendom, the chief pontiff, to marry a second time is unlawful. How pleasing must holiness be to God, when even His enemy affects it! —not, of course, as having any affinity with anything good, but as contumeliously affecting what is pleasing to God the Lord.

Chapter VIII. —Conclusion.

For, concerning the honors which widowhood enjoys in the sight of God, there is a brief summary in one saying of His through the prophet: "Do thou justly to the widow and to the orphan; and come ye, let us reason, saith the Lord." These two names, left to the care of the divine mercy, in proportion as they are destitute of human aid, the Father of all undertakes to defend. Look how the widow's benefactor is put on a level with the widow herself, whose champion shall "reason with the Lord!" Not to virgins, I take it, is so great a gift given. Although in *their* case perfect integrity and entire sanctity shall have the nearest vision of the face of God, yet the widow has a task more toilsome, because it is easy not to crave after that which you know not, and to turn away from what you have never had to regret. More glorious is the continence which is aware of its own right, which knows what it has seen. The virgin may possibly be held the happier, but the *widow* the more hardly tasked; the former in that she has always kept "the good," the latter in that she has found "the good for herself." In the former it is grace, in the latter virtue, that is crowned. For some things there are which are of the divine liberality, some of our own working. The indulgences granted by the Lord are regulated by their own grace; the things which are objects of man's striving are attained by earnest pursuit. Pursue earnestly, therefore, the virtue of continence, which is modesty's agent; industry, which allows not women to be "wanderers;" frugality, which scorns the world. Follow companies and conversations worthy of God, mindful of that short verse, sanctified by the apostle's quotation of it, "Ill interviews good morals do corrupt." Talkative, idle, winebibbing, curious tent-fellows, do the very greatest hurt to the purpose of widow-hood. Through talkativeness there creep in words unfriendly to modesty; through idleness they seduce one from strictness; through winebibbing they insinuate any and every evil; through curiosity they convey a spirit of rivalry in lust. Not one of such women knows how to speak of the good of single-husband- hood; for their "god," as the apostle says, "is their belly;" and so, too, what is neighbor to the belly.

These considerations, dearest fellow-servant, I commend to you thus early, handled throughout superfluously indeed, after the apostle, but likely to prove a solace to you, in that (if so it shall turn out) you will cherish my memory in them.

Book II.

Chapter I.—Reasons Which Led to the Writing of This Second Book.

Very lately, best beloved fellow-servant in the Lord, I, as my ability permitted, entered for your benefit at some length into the question what course is to be followed by a holy woman when her marriage has (in whatever way) been brought to an end. Let us now turn our attention to the next best advice, in regard of human infirmity; admonished hereto by the examples of certain, who, when an opportunity for the practice of continence has been offered them, by divorce, or by the decease of the husband, have not only thrown away the opportunity of attaining so great a good, but not even in their remarriage have chosen to be mindful of the rule that "above all they marry in the Lord." And thus my mind has been thrown into confusion, in the fear that, having exhorted you myself to perseverance in single husband hood and widowhood, I may now, by the mention of precipitate marriages, put "an occasion of falling" in your way. But if you are perfect in wisdom, you know, of course, that the course which is the more useful is the course which you must keep. But, inasmuch as that course is difficult, and not without its embarrassments, and on this account is the highest aim of (widowed) life, I have paused somewhat (in my urging you to it); nor would there have been any causes for my recurring to that point also in addressing you, had I not by this time taken up a still graver solicitude. For the nobler is the continence of the flesh which ministers to widowhood, the more pardonable a thing it seems if it be not persevered in. For it is then when things are difficult that their pardon is easy. But in as far as marrying "in the Lord" is permissible, as being within our power, so far more culpable is it *not* to observe that which you *can* observe. Add to this the fact that the apostle, with regard to widows and the unmarried, *advises* them to remain permanently in that state, when he says, "But I desire all to persevere in (imitation of) my example:" but touching marrying "in the Lord," he no longer *advises*, but plainly *bids*. Therefore, in this case especially, if we do not obey, we run a risk, because one may with more impunity neglect an "advice" than an "order;" in that the former springs from *counsel*, and is proposed to the *will* (for acceptance or rejection): the other descends from *authority*, and is bound to *necessity*.

In the former case, to disregard appears *liberty*, in the latter, *contumacy*.

Chapter II. —Of the Apostle's Meaning in 1 Cor. VII. 12–14.

Therefore, when in these days a certain woman removed her marriage from the pale of the Church, and united herself to a Gentile, and when I remembered that this had in days gone by been done by others: wondering at either their own waywardness or else the double-dealing of their advisers, in that there is no scripture which holds forth a license of this deed, — "I wonder," said I, "whether they flatter themselves on the ground of that passage of the first (Epistle) to the Corinthians, where it is written: If any of the brethren has an unbelieving wife, and she consents to the matrimony, let him not dismiss her; similarly, let not a believing woman, married to an unbeliever, if she finds her husband agreeable (to their continued union), dismiss him: for the unbelieving husband is sanctified by the believing wife, and the unbelieving wife by the believing husband; else were your children unclean." It may be that, by understanding *generally* this monition regarding *married* believers, they think that license is granted (thereby) to marry even *un*believers. God forbid that he who thus interprets (the passage) be *wittingly* ensnaring himself! But it is manifest that this scripture points to those believers who may have been found by the grace of God in (the state of) Gentile matrimony; according to the words themselves: "If," it says, "any believer *has* an unbelieving wife;" it does not say, "*takes* an unbelieving wife." It shows that it is the duty of one who, already living in marriage with an unbelieving woman, has presently been by the grace of God converted, to continue with his wife; for this reason, to be sure, in order that no one, after attaining to faith, should think that he must turn away from a woman who is now in some sense an "alien" and "stranger." Accordingly, he subjoins withal a

reason, that "we are called *in peace* unto the Lord God;" and that "the unbeliever may, through the use of matrimony, *be gained* by the believer." The very closing sentence of the period confirms (the supposition) that this is thus to be understood. "As each," it says, "is called by the Lord, so let him persevere." But it is *Gentiles* who "are called," I take it, not *believers*. But if he had been pronouncing *absolutely*, (in the words under discussion,) touching the marriage of believers merely, (then) had he (virtually) given to saints a permission to marry promiscuously. If, however, he had given such a permission, he would never have subjoined a declaration so diverse from and contrary to his own permission, saying: "The woman, when her husband is dead, is free: let her marry whom she wishes, *only in the Lord*." Here, at all events, there is no need for reconsidering; for what there *might* have been reconsideration about, the Spirit has oracularly declared. For fear we should make an ill use of what he says, "Let her marry whom she wishes," he has added, "only in the Lord," that is, in the name of the Lord, which is, undoubtedly, "to a Christian."
That "Holy Spirit," therefore, who prefers that widows and unmarried women should persevere in their integrity, who exhorts us to a copy of himself, prescribes no other manner of repeating marriage except "in the Lord:" to this condition alone does he concede the foregoing of continence. "Only," he says, "in the Lord:" he has added to his law a weight— "*only*." Utter that word with what tone and manner you may, it is weighty: it both bids and advises; both enjoins and exhorts; both asks and threatens. It is a concise, brief sentence; and by its own very brevity, eloquent. Thus is the divine voice wont (to speak), that you may instantly understand, instantly observe. For who but could understand that the apostle foresaw many dangers and wounds to faith in marriages of this kind, which he prohibits? and that he took precaution, in the first place, against the defilement of holy flesh in Gentile flesh? At this point someone says, "What, then, is the difference between him who is chosen by the Lord to Himself in (the state of) Gentile

marriage, and him who was of old (that is, before marriage) a believer, that they should not be equally cautious for their flesh? —whereas the one is kept from marriage with an unbeliever, the other bidden to continue in it. Why, if we are defiled by a Gentile, is not the one disjoined, just as the other is not bound?" I will answer, if the Spirit give (me ability); alleging, before all (other arguments), that the Lord holds it more pleasing that matrimony should not be contracted, than that it should at all be dissolved: in short, divorce He prohibits, except for the cause of fornication; but continence He commends. Let the one, therefore, have the necessity of continuing; the other, further, even the power of not marrying. Secondly, if, according to the Scripture, they who shall be "apprehended" by the faith in (the state of) Gentile marriage are not defiled (thereby) for this reason, that, together with themselves, others also are sanctified: without doubt, they who have been sanctified *before* marriage, if they commingle themselves with "strange flesh," cannot sanctify that (flesh) in (union with) which they were not "apprehended." The grace of God, moreover, sanctifies that which it *finds*. Thus, what has not been able to be sanctified is unclean; what is unclean has no part with the holy, unless to defile and slay it by its own (nature).

Chapter III. —Remarks on Some of the "Dangers and Wounds" Referred to in the Preceding Chapter.

If these things are so, it is certain that believers contracting marriages with Gentiles are guilty of fornication, and are to be excluded from all communication with the brotherhood, in accordance with the letter of the apostle, who says that "with persons of that kind there is to be no taking of food even." Or shall we "in that day" produce (our) marriage certificates before the Lord's tribunal, and allege that a marriage such as He Himself has forbidden has been duly contracted? What is prohibited (in the passage just referred to) is not "adultery;" it is not "fornication." The admission of a strange man (to your couch) less violates "the temple of God," less commingles "the members of Christ" with the members of an adulteress. So far as I know, "we are not our own, but bought with a price;" and what kind of price? The blood of God. In hurting this flesh of ours, therefore, we hurt Him directly. What did that man mean who said that "to wed a 'stranger' was indeed a sin, but a very small one?" whereas in other cases (setting aside the injury done to the flesh which pertains to the Lord) *every* voluntary sin against the Lord is *great*. For, in as far as there was a power of avoiding it, in so far is it burdened with the charge of contumacy.

Let us now recount the other dangers or wounds (as I have said) to faith, foreseen by the apostle; most grievous not to the flesh merely, but likewise to the spirit too. For who would doubt that faith undergoes a daily process of obliteration by unbelieving intercourse? "Evil confabulations corrupt good morals;" how much more fellowship of life, and indivisible intimacy! Any and every believing woman must of necessity obey God. And how can she serve two lords—the Lord, and her husband—a Gentile to boot? For in obeying a Gentile she will carry out Gentile practices, —personal attractiveness, dressing of the head, worldly elegancies, baser blandishments, the very secrets even of matrimony tainted: not, as among the saints, where the duties of the sex are discharged with honor (shown) to the very necessity (which makes them incumbent), with modesty and temperance, as beneath the eyes of God.

Chapter IV. —Of the Hindrances Which an Unbelieving Husband Puts in His Wife's Way.

But let her see to (the question) how she discharges her duties to her husband. To the Lord, at all events, she is unable to give satisfaction according to the requirements of discipline;

having at her side a servant of the devil, *his* lord's agent for hindering the pursuits and duties of believers: so that if a station is to be kept, the husband at daybreak makes an appointment with his wife to meet him at the baths; if there are fasts to be observed, the husband that same day holds a convivial banquet; if a charitable expedition has to be made, never is family business more urgent. For who would suffer his wife, for the sake of visiting the brethren, to go round from street to street to other men's, and indeed to all the poorer, cottages? Who will willingly bear her being taken from his side by nocturnal convocations, if need so be? Who, finally, will without anxiety endure her absence all the night long at the paschal solemnities? Who will, without some suspicion of his own, dismiss her to attend that Lord's Supper which they defame? Who will suffer her to creep into prison to kiss a martyr's bonds? nay, truly, to meet any one of the brethren to exchange the kiss? to offer water for the saints' feet? to snatch (somewhat for them) from her food, from her cup? to yearn (after them)? to have (them) in her mind? If a pilgrim brother arrives, what hospitality for him in an alien home? If bounty is to be distributed to any, the granaries, the storehouses, are foreclosed.

Chapter V.—Of Sin and Danger Incurred Even with a "Tolerant" Husband.

"But some husband does endure our (practices), and not annoy us." *Here*, therefore, there is a sin; in that Gentiles *know* our (practices); in that we are subject to the privity of the unjust; in that it is thanks to them that we do any (good) work. He who "endures" (a thing) cannot be ignorant of it; or else, if he is kept in ignorance because he does *not* endure (it), he is feared. But since Scripture commands each of two things—namely, that we work for the Lord without the privity of any second person, and without pressure upon ourselves, it matters not in which quarter you sin; whether in regard to your husband's privity, if he be tolerant, or else in regard of your own affliction in avoiding his *in*tolerance. "Cast not," saith He, "your pearls to swine, lest they trample them to pieces, and turn round and overturn you also." "Your pearls" are the distinctive marks of even your daily conversation. The more care you take to conceal them, the more liable to suspicion you will make them, and the more exposed to the grasp of Gentile curiosity. Shall you escape notice when you sign your bed, (or) your body; when you blow away some impurity; when even by night you rise to pray? Will you not be thought to be engaged in some work of magic? Will not your husband know what it is which you secretly taste before (taking) any food? and if he knows it to be bread, does he not believe it to be *that* (bread) which it is *said* to be? And will every (husband), ignorant of the reason of these things, simply endure them, without murmuring, without suspicion whether it be bread or poison? Some, (it is true,) *do* endure (them); but it is that they may trample on, that they may make sport of such women; whose secrets they keep in reserve against the danger which they believe in, in case they ever chance to be hurt: they do endure (wives), whose dowries, by casting in their teeth their (Christian) name, they make the wages of silence; while they threaten them, forsooth, with a suit before some spy as arbitrator! which most women, not foreseeing, have been wont to discover either by the extortion of their property, or else by the loss of their faith.

Chapter VI. —Danger of Having to Take Part in Heathenish Rites, and Revels.

The handmaid of God dwells amid alien labors; and among these (labors), on all the memorial days of demons, at all solemnities of kings, at the beginning of the year, at the beginning of the month, she will be agitated by the odor of incense. And she will have to go forth (from her house) by a gate wreathed with laurel, and hung with lanterns, as from some new consistory of public lusts; she will have to sit with her husband ofttimes in club meetings, oft-times in taverns; and, wont as she was formerly to minister to the "saints," will sometimes have to minister to the "unjust." And will she not hence recognize a prejudgment of her own damnation, in that she *tends* them whom (formerly) she was expecting to *judge*? whose hand will she yearn after? of whose cup will she partake? What will her husband sing to her, or she to her husband? From the tavern, I suppose, she who sups upon God will hear somewhat! From hell what mention of God (arises)? What invocation of Christ? Where are the fosterings of faith by the interspersion of the Scriptures (in conversation)? Where the Spirit? where refreshment? where the divine benediction? All things are strange, all inimical, all condemned; aimed by the Evil One for the attrition of salvation!

Chapter VII. —The Case of a Heathen Whose Wife is Converted After Marriage with Him Very Different, and Much More Hopeful.

If these things may happen to those women also who, having attained the faith while in (the state of) Gentile matrimony, continue in that state, still they are excused, as having been "apprehended by God" in these very circumstances; and they are *bidden* to persevere in their married state, and are sanctified, and have hope of "making a gain" held out to them. "If, then, a marriage of this kind (contracted *before* conversion) stands ratified before God, why should not (one contracted *after* conversion) too go prosperously forward, so as not to be thus harassed by pressures, and straits, and hindrances, and defilements, having already (as it has) the partial sanction of divine grace? "Because, on the one hand, the wife in the former case, called *from among* the Gentiles to the exercise of some eminent heavenly virtue, is, by the visible proofs of some marked (divine) regard, a terror to her Gentile husband, so as to make him less ready to annoy her, less active in laying snares for her, less diligent in playing the spy over her. He has felt "mighty works;" he has seen experimental evidences; he knows her changed for the better: thus even he himself is, by his fear, a candidate for God. Thus men of this kind, with regard to whom the grace of God has established a familiar intimacy, are more easily "gained." But, on the other hand, to descend into forbidden ground unsolicited and spontaneously, is (quite) another thing. Things which are not pleasing to the Lord, of course offend the Lord, are of course introduced by the Evil One. A sign hereof is this fact, that it is *wooers* only who find the Christian name pleasing; and, accordingly, some heathen men are found not to shrink in horror from Christian women, just in order to exterminate them, to wrest them away, to exclude them from the faith. So long as marriage of this kind is procured by the Evil One, but condemned by God, you have a reason why you need not doubt that it can in no case be carried to a prosperous end.

Chapter VIII. —Arguments Drawn Even from Heathenish Laws to Discountenance Marriage with Unbelievers. The Happiness of Union Between Partners in the Faith Enlarged on in Conclusion.

Let us further inquire, as if we were in very deed inquisitors of divine sentences, whether they be lawfully (thus condemned). Even among the nations, do not all the strictest lords and most tenacious of discipline interdict their own slaves from marrying out of their own house? —in order, of course, that they may not run into lascivious excess, desert their duties, purvey their lords' goods to strangers. Yet, further, have not (the nations) decided that such women as have, after their lords' formal warning, persisted in intercourse with other men's slaves, may be claimed as slaves? Shall earthly disciplines be held more strict than heavenly prescripts; so that *Gentile* women, if united to strangers, lose their liberty; *ours* conjoin to themselves the devil's slaves, and continue in their (former) position? Forsooth, they will deny that any formal warning has been given them by the Lord through His own apostle!

What am I to fasten on as the cause of this madness, except the weakness of faith, ever prone to the concupiscence of worldly joys? —which, indeed, is chiefly found among the wealthier; for the more any is rich, and inflated with the name of "matron," the more capacious house does she require for her burdens, as it were a field wherein ambition may run its course. To such the churches look paltry. A rich man is a difficult thing (to find) in the house of God; and if such a one is (found there), difficult (is it to find such) unmarried. What, then, are they to do? Whence but from the devil are they to seek a husband apt for maintaining their sedan, and their mules, and their hair-curlers of outlandish stature? A Christian, even although rich, would perhaps not afford (all) these. Set before yourself, I beg of you, the examples of Gentiles. Most Gentile women, noble in extraction and wealthy in property, unite themselves indiscriminately with the ignoble and the mean, sought out for themselves for luxurious, or mutilated for licentious, purposes. Some take up with their own freedmen and slaves, despising public opinion, provided they may but have (husbands) from whom to fear no impediment to their own liberty. To a Christian believer it is irksome to wed a believer inferior to herself in estate, destined as she will be to have her wealth augmented in the person of a poor husband! For if it is "the poor," not the rich, "whose are the kingdoms of the heavens," the rich will find more in the poor (than she brings him, or than she would in the rich). She will be dowered with an ampler dowry from the goods of him who is rich in God. Let her be on an equality with him on earth, who in the heavens will perhaps not be so. Is there need for doubt, and inquiry, and repeated deliberation, whether he whom God has entrusted with His own property is fit for dotal endowments? Whence are we to find (words) enough fully to tell the happiness of that marriage

which the Church cements, and the oblation confirms, and the benediction signs and seals;
(which) angels carry back the news of (to heaven), (which) the Father holds for ratified? For even on earth children do not rightly and lawfully wed without their fathers' consent. What kind of yoke is that of two believers, (partakers) of one hope, one desire, one discipline, one and the same service? Both (are) brethren, both fellow servants, no difference of spirit or of flesh; nay, (they are) truly "two in one flesh." Where the flesh is one, one is the spirit too. Together they pray, together prostrate themselves, together perform their fasts; mutually teaching, mutually exhorting, mutually sustaining. Equally (are they) both (found) in the Church of God; equally at the banquet of God; equally in straits, in persecutions, in refreshments. Neither hides (ought) from the other; neither shuns the other; neither is troublesome to the other. The sick is visited, the indigent relieved, with freedom. Alms (are given) without (danger of ensuing) torment; sacrifices (attended) without scruple; daily diligence (discharged) without impediment: (there is) no stealthy signing, no trembling greeting, no mute benediction. Between the two echo psalms and hymns; and they mutually challenge each other which shall better chant to their Lord. Such things when Christ sees and hears, He joys. To these He sends His own peace. Where two (are), there withal (is) He Himself. Where He (is), there the Evil One is not. These are the things which that utterance of the apostle has, beneath its brevity, left to be understood by us. These things, if need shall be, suggest to your own mind. By these turn yourself away from the examples of some. To marry *otherwise* is, to believers, not "lawful;" is not "expedient."

Elucidation.

(Marriage lawful, p. 39.)

St. Peter was a married apostle, and the traditions of his wife which connect her married life with Rome itself render it most surprising that those who claim to be St. Peter's successors should denounce the marriage of the clergy as if it were crime. The touching story, borrowed from Clement of Alexandria, is related by Eusebius. "And will they," says Clement, "reject even the apostles? Peter and Philip, indeed, had children; Philip also gave his daughters in marriage to husbands; and Paul does not demur, in a certain Epistle, to mention his own wife, whom he did not take about with him, in order to expedite his ministry, the better." Of St. Peter and his wife, Eusebius subjoins, "Such was the marriage of these blessed ones, and such was their perfect affection."

The Easterns to this day perpetuate the marriage of the clergy, and enjoin it; but unmarried men only are chosen to be bishops. Even Rome relaxes her discipline for the *Uniats*, and hundreds of her priesthood, therefore, live in honorable marriage. Thousands live in secret marriage, but their wives are dishonored as "concubines." It was not till the eleventh century that the celibate was enforced. In England it was *never* successfully imposed; and, though the "priest's *leman*" was not called his *wife* (to the disgrace of the whole system), she was yet honored (see Chaucer), and often carried herself too proudly.

The enormous evils of an enforced celibacy need not here be remarked upon. The history of *Sacerdotal Celibacy*, by Henry C. Lea of Philadelphia, is compendious, and can be readily procured by all who wish to understand what it is that this treatise of Tertullian's orthodoxy may best be used to teach; viz., that we must not be wiser than God, even in our zeal for His service.

www.ingramcontent.com/pod-product-compliance
Lightning Source LLC
Chambersburg PA
CBHW071015120726
47910CB00004B/1534

* 9 7 8 1 6 4 3 7 3 0 9 9 8 *